PLANET OCEAN

WHY WE ALL NEED A HEALTHY OCEAN

Patricia Newman

Photographs by Annie Crawley

MILLBROOK PRESS • MINNEAPOLIS

To Elise, Scott, Megan, Mia, David, Greg, Jacob, and Daniel—the future
of our ocean
—P.N.

To my mom Harriet Pergande, my Dive Team, and everyone who speaks
up for our Planet Ocean!
—A.C.

Back cover caption: Photographer Steve Woods captured this shot of Annie in action filming a baby humpback whale.
Jacket flap caption: Patricia Newman (*center left*) and Annie Crawley (*center right*) with Annie's Dive Team in Seattle,
Washington, photographed by Raechel Romero.
Title page caption: Hooded nudibranchs (*Melibe leonina*) in an eelgrass bed.

Millbrook Press™
An imprint of Lerner Publishing Group, Inc.
241 First Avenue North
Minneapolis, MN 55401 USA

For reading levels and more information, look up this title at www.lernerbooks.com.

Additional photo credits: Tom Gruber, p. 8 (top); Hergen Spalink, p. 8 (bottom); Harold Bailey, p. 31; Terry Keffler, p. 52 (top).

Main body text set in Avenir LT Pro. Typeface provided by Linotype AG.

Library of Congress Cataloging-in-Publication Data

Names: Newman, Patricia, 1958– author. | Crawley, Annie, underwater photographer. | Millbrook Press.
Title: Planet ocean : why we all need a healthy ocean / Patricia Newman ; [photographs by Annie Crawley].
Description: Minneapolis : Millbrook Press, 2021. | Includes webography. | Includes bibliographical references and
    index. | Audience: Ages 9–14 years | Audience: Grades 4–6 | Summary: "Travel beneath the waves and visit three
    distinct parts of the ocean to examine climate change, pollution, and sustainability. And find out what you can do
    to protect the health of the ocean!" —Provided by publisher.
Identifiers: LCCN 2019055146 (print) | LCCN 2019055147 (ebook) | ISBN 9781541581210 (Library Binding) |
    ISBN 9781728401515 (eBook)
Subjects: LCSH: Ocean—Juvenile literature. | Oceanography. | Marine sciences.
Classification: LCC GC21.5 .N49 2021 (print) | LCC GC21.5 (ebook) | DDC 551.46—dc23

LC record available at https://lccn.loc.gov/2019055146
LC ebook record available at https://lccn.loc.gov/2019055147

Manufactured in the United States of America
1-47320-47947-8/26/2020

For more digital content,
download a QR code reader
app on your phone, tablet, or
other smart device. Then scan
the QR codes throughout the
book to dive below the surface
with Annie Crawley and see
the ocean as she sees it.

CONTENTS

INTRODUCTION
THE MAPS ARE WRONG **4**

CHAPTER 1
THE CORAL TRIANGLE: CITIES OF THE SEA **10**

CHAPTER 2
THE SALISH SEA: OUR CONNECTION IS REAL **22**

CHAPTER 3
THE ARCTIC: THE TOP OF THE WORLD **32**

CHAPTER 4
IT'S YOUR TURN: THE OCEAN'S STORY IS OUR STORY . . .**44**

A NOTE FROM THE AUTHOR AND THE PHOTOGRAPHER 54

GLOSSARY 56

SOURCE NOTES 57

SELECTIONS FROM OUR BIBLIOGRAPHY 60

DIVE INTO THESE OCEAN BOOKS 60

SURFERS WELCOME 61

INDEX 62

INTRODUCTION
THE MAPS ARE WRONG

WHAT POPS INTO YOUR MIND WHEN YOU HEAR THE WORD *OCEAN*? Sharks? Rolling waves? Seagulls? Or maybe salt water, kelp, or coral?

We've all seen the five "oceans" on world maps, but the maps haven't been telling us the whole truth. The truth is we have only one ocean. It's all connected. And most maps make the ocean look smaller than the land. Planet Earth is actually about 70 percent ocean and only 30 percent land. A better name for it would be Planet Ocean.

Although scientists have studied our ocean for nearly 130 years, much of it remains unexplored because of its colossal size. Every day scientists learn something new about the secrets of the deep. The ocean promises an enormous variety of awe-inspiring life, from microscopic bacteria to aquatic plants to fish of every size to the blue whale, the largest animal on the planet. Every single life-form plays an important role in keeping the ocean healthy.

The ocean is also the engine of *our* existence. The sea's bounty feeds more than three billion

The ocean stores 97 percent of our water. Ice caps store 2 percent, and rivers, lakes, and streams store 1 percent.

people. Salmon, shrimp, clams, squid, oysters, tuna, and crab regularly appear on our dinner plates. And ocean plants use the sun's energy to simultaneously make their own food and more than half of the oxygen we breathe, even if we don't live near the coast. Every drop of water we drink starts with the ocean. The sun's hot rays cause surface water to evaporate as water vapor, which condenses into clouds. Inside clouds, water drops form. These drops fall as rain, snow, sleet, or hail. They soak into the ground and swell our lakes and wells, feed our rivers, or freeze as glaciers and polar ice. Water equals life for plants, animals, and us.

But these facts only scratch the surface. We know more about outer space than we do the mysteries of our ocean. Crazy, right?

Without the ocean, we simply wouldn't *be*, yet many of us live apart from it. Some of us have never even seen it. Others have merely visited on vacation. Even those who live on the coast rarely consider our connection to it. We may admire the pounding surf and think we appreciate the ocean, but the core of our unbreakable connection lies underwater within its variety of habitats and complex food webs.

To investigate how the ocean's story is our story, underwater explorer Annie Crawley will guide us on a deep dive to three of her favorite ocean regions: the Coral Triangle of Indonesia, the Salish Sea in the Pacific Northwest, and the Arctic at the top of the world. Even though these three unique areas are thousands of miles apart, they are part of one world ocean connected by marine life and circulating currents heedless of the boundary lines on our maps. Human habits also link these regions, especially overfishing and pollution from plastic, noise, excess carbon, and runoff from our streets.

Ocean currents have always gathered floating driftwood and feathers. Lately, currents also collect tons of plastic and move it around the ocean.

"I know how important the ocean is to our daily lives, how fragile it is, and how much we're changing it. I want kids and teens to speak up for our ocean."
—Annie Crawley

With Annie, we'll not only explore the ocean's surface but also the magical world beneath. Annie is a certified master scuba diving instructor with nearly thirty years of underwater experience. Some say she's a mermaid. "I have this deep connection and this passion for our underwater world and it started with my first breaths underwater," she says. "When I slip through the thin blue line that separates sea and air, I'm home. If you look closely behind my ears, you'll see faint lines where my gills used to be." Her mischievous grin makes us want to believe.

As an award-winning photographer and filmmaker, Annie uses images to tell our ocean's story and to urge us to become a voice for the sea. Through her lens we'll dive deep to uncover the true story of the beating blue heart of our planet—as well as the threats it faces and how those threats influence us.

Meet Annie Crawley, also known as Ocean Annie.

snorkel for breathing near the surface

regulator to breathe air from the tank

a mask to see clearly underwater

hoses carry air from air tank to equipment

hand signals used by divers around the world

compass to navigate

computer for measuring depth, time, and remaining air

dive light to see color

drysuit, hood, and gloves for warmth

fins to swim like a fish

DISCOVER SCUBA: ELISE FOOT PUCHALSKI

Annie teaches many people to dive, including teens and children as young as ten years old. Elise learned to dive at the age of twelve at Annie's summer camp and is now a member of the Dive Team. "Underwater you enter a whole new world," Elise says. "Diving is my favorite sport. My friends think I'm an ocean expert."

CHAPTER 1
THE CORAL TRIANGLE:
CITIES OF THE SEA

WELCOME TO THE CORAL TRIANGLE, HOME TO MORE THAN ONE-THIRD OF THE WORLD'S CORAL. Coral reefs have been the foundation of the marine world for four hundred million years. Annie calls them the cities of the sea. Millions of animals dart around colorful reefs and hide in their crevices, including turtles, clown fish, eels, octopuses, angelfish, lobsters, sea stars, and reef sharks. Reefs are busy, bustling places where one-fourth of all ocean species spend time at some point in their lives.

The staggering biodiversity of coral reefs makes them critical to marine and human life. Reef fish feed billions of people and are as important to the global food supply as crops and farm animals are on land. Coral reefs dampen waves and protect coastlines from erosion. Scientists even make medicines from coral and other reef dwellers to treat cancer and heart disease. Because coral reefs are some of the most astonishing places on the planet, they drive a multibillion-dollar tourist industry that employs millions of people.

Annie describes coral reefs as creativity unleashed. "No one could have prepared me for the electric blue of staghorn coral; the reef's pinks and purples made of dreams; the flamboyant cuttlefish that turn red, yellow, and white when threatened."

But humans have put coral reefs in terrible danger with unsustainable fishing practices, mining, plastic pollution, and excess carbon. "The ocean is us," Annie says. "Its beauty and its pain. And the best way to understand that is through our stories."

Take the plunge with Annie to visit Indonesia's rainbow sea.

Angelique Batuna, Annie's longtime friend and dive buddy, has witnessed many of these problems in her native Indonesia, a nation of seventeen thousand islands within the heart of the Coral Triangle.

"I grew up at the ocean. It's where my heart is," Angelique says. "I was thirteen when my father took me diving for the first time. It was an amazing feeling!" Now the ocean is Angelique's life. She and her family own two dive resorts and one scuba diving center that provide jobs for nearly two hundred people in North Sulawesi Province.

By saving coral reefs, Angelique saves creatures like manta rays.

"The ocean is what we promote to tourists from Europe, the US, all over the world," she says.

When a Chinese mining company arrived in Indonesia in 2011 to dig iron ore out of Bangka Island, Angelique became concerned. Iron ore is used to make steel, and its value is second only to oil in our global economy. Mining companies blast, drill, and dig the ore out of the ground, polluting the water and destroying vital coral reefs and mangrove habitats. Mangrove trees grow in seawater and protect the coast from storms, clean chemicals out of the water, stop sediments from damaging corals, and store carbon. Without mangroves, the island and its reefs would be exposed.

"The island would be stripped empty with nothing left," Angelique says. "This place is our livelihood. We've been here forever. We're not going anywhere."

After the mining company ripped out the mangroves along the shore, Angelique organized fellow business owners, friends, and villagers to prevent the company from doing any more damage. In 2017 they convinced the Indonesian government to cancel the company's permit before it stripped any iron ore from the ground.

Local people are working to replant mangroves to once again protect the shoreline.

Next, Angelique turned her attention to fish bombing, once a popular way to catch fish in Indonesia. Fishermen tossed grenade-like bottle bombs into the water. The bombs exploded, killing or stunning dozens of fish, which made them easy to gather. But the bombs also destroyed coral reefs, endangering the ecosystem and the islanders' way of life. "It was an easy way to fish," Angelique says, "but it was shortsighted." Although fish bombing was outlawed in 2004, the law is difficult to enforce in a nation of seventeen thousand islands.

To make room for the ships that would haul ore away for processing, the mining company removed mangrove trees from Bangka Island. Angelique (*right*) helped close the mine.

So, Angelique decided to educate her staff. She hired a coral expert to explain the fascinating lives of corals. Her staff could then educate their families and resort guests about these amazing animals in their own backyard.

Together, they learned that millions of tiny animals called polyps make up a single reef so large it can often be seen from space. As polyps grow, they absorb carbonate ion from the water to make calcium carbonate, which gives the reef its bony structure. On the outside, polyps coat themselves in a layer of mucus that acts as a shield against disease. On the inside live tiny plants called zooxanthellae (zo-a-zan-THEL-ee). The zooxanthellae make 95 percent of the polyps' food by photosynthesis—converting sunlight and carbon dioxide into energy. And every night, corals put on a show. Stinging tentacles bloom from the polyps to capture tiny floating animals for a remarkable midnight feast. Meanwhile, the polyps fight the world's slowest war as they battle with one another for space on the reef, millimeter by millimeter.

"I admire Angelique because she's conservation driven," Annie says. "When we learn the ecology of the region, we understand how everything relates and have a greater respect for it. When we respect an ecosystem, we work hard to find solutions to its problems."

Life flourishes on a healthy coral reef.

Carbon pollution poses another serious threat to corals. Every living thing needs carbon to thrive—trees, whales, people, sharks, roses, carrots. The list is endless. But too much of a good thing becomes deadly.

We use the term *climate change* to describe carbon pollution, but most of us think only about how it affects our land and our air. We tend to forget climate change also affects the ocean. When we burn fossil fuels such as gasoline, carbon dioxide levels rise in the air *and* in seawater. Scientists estimate about one-third of the carbon dioxide in the air dissolves in the ocean every year. All this extra carbon dioxide creates two dangerous problems for marine life and us: more acid in the water and higher water temperatures.

When carbon dioxide dissolves in seawater, a chemical reaction called ocean acidification takes place. Water and carbon dioxide combine and form an acid. The acid immediately releases hydrogen ions, particles that race through the water searching for carbonate ion—the very same stuff corals need to grow. Corals are confined to their reefs and don't move around much, but hydrogen ions zip all over the place. It doesn't take much imagination to guess the winner in the battle for carbonate ion. The hydrogen ions trap available carbonate ion before coral polyps can.

A dead reef devastated by coral bleaching, ocean acidification, or both.

Without enough carbonate ion, corals grow slowly and build weak reefs that can wash away in rough seas. If the amount of carbonate ion drops too low, the reefs Angelique works so hard to save might even dissolve.

What about the carbon dioxide that doesn't dissolve in the ocean? It harms our sea too. Some of the sunlight that reaches our planet normally bounces back toward space. But carbon dioxide traps this heat in our atmosphere, which increases the temperature of seawater all over the world. Remember the zooxanthellae inside coral polyps? Warm water causes them to produce too much oxygen during photosynthesis. This extra oxygen is so poisonous that the polyps spit out their zooxanthellae. Without zooxanthellae to make food, the polyps starve. Without zooxanthellae, the polyps whiten (bleach). Sometimes corals recover from bleaching if cold-water currents return and new zooxanthellae move in. Sometimes they don't.

In recent years, half of the corals in Australia's Great Barrier Reef bleached and starved in warming water. More than 60 percent of the coral in the Maldives is struggling to survive after bleaching. Curiously, the corals of Indonesia where Angelique lives did not bleach or starve. Scientists suspect that a cold ocean current flowing through the area makes Indonesian corals hardier.

Warming ocean temperatures also melt faraway ice in the Arctic. Melting ice raises the water level along our coasts and floods sandy beaches such as Angelique's. A few years ago, she built a seawall to protect her resort, but it's no longer tall enough to block the relentless rise of water. Waves as tall as 10 feet (3 m) crash over the wall and flood the area beyond it. "We're moving the resort back," Angelique says.

Millions of animals call coral reefs home, including the pygmy seahorse, which is smaller than your pinkie fingernail.

"Angelique is lucky because she has room to move," Annie says. "But think about the millions of people who live along the coastline around the world—not only island nations, but coastal cities in the US." Every year since 2008, about twenty-four million people in Africa, Asia, South America, and the US have been forced to leave their homes as climate refugees. Many more will follow.

Plastic pollution creates yet another severe threat to the health of coral reefs. Drifting plastic bags, plastic fishing nets, and plastic fishing line become caught on coral and block the sunlight zooxanthellae need to feed the polyps. And when plastic touches coral, it damages the mucous protecting coral from disease.

Even though the Coral Triangle may be far from our homes, its beautiful abundance sustains us. Pollution and warming seas threaten that abundance. "As a diver and conservationist, Angelique understands this," Annie says. "Without corals, fish will leave to find food elsewhere. And without fish, the fishing and tourism industries will collapse. Waves will erode the coastline. People around the world will be left hungry, unprotected, and unemployed." When we understand our connection to the coral ecosystem, we begin to respect it. And with respect comes the hard work of protecting it.

Take the Plastic Pollution 30-Day Challenge.

MAKING WAVES: HELEN PANANGGUNG AND THE CHILDREN

The children in the village of Pintu Kota Kecil in Indonesia know all about plastic pollution. Ocean currents deposit piles of the stuff on their beach every day. At first, they were angry. Then, in 2018, their anger morphed into action. Green Guru Helen Pananggung lives in the village and inspires them to fight back against ocean plastic. "I believe if no one starts, then nothing happens," Helen says. "It's difficult to find a clean beach. Plastic always comes in on the tide."

The children go to work every Sunday—chatting and smiling—as the first line of defense in a community effort to simultaneously get rid of plastic and create jobs. They wade through the shallows and walk the muddy sand still wet from high tide. They stuff plastic pieces, big and small, into discarded plastic bags repurposed for beach cleanups.

Some of the plastic they collect becomes eco-bricks, which were used to build the community's Trash Bank. The Trash Bank recycles waste plastic into 3D printer filament, and the jewelry boxes, bowls, handles, and toys that community members make. Many of these items are sold in resort gift shops, and the money then returns to the community.

As Helen watches the children, her eyes flood with tears. They face overwhelming odds. Every tide brings a fresh wave of trash. "Many people don't care and think it's not their responsibility," she says. "I want the kids to learn how important it is to save the place we live so one day we still have a place to live. Here is a message from the children in my village to all of you wherever you are:

"Stop buang sampah di laut karena laut bukan tempat sampah.

"Stop throwing trash in the sea because the sea is not a trash can."

On her first-ever scuba dive, Nicole (*right*) swam over a coral-replanting project at a destroyed reef. "When I saw the coral project, I knew I had to follow this path."

Another dive buddy of Annie's is one of the people doing some of this hard work. Ocean gardener Nicole Helgason plants living coral fragments on damaged reefs in the Coral Triangle to restore them to their natural beauty and usefulness. She shows local people how to rebuild reefs to help support a healthy habitat near their villages for fishing and tourism.

Nicole also shares her passion for corals in a series of videos that teach fellow divers how to identify and protect them. She encourages divers to float above corals to avoid touching or

kicking them with fins. These simple scuba and snorkeling techniques give delicate corals a chance when so many other things are working against them. Nicole's fascination with corals also rubs off on local children, many of whom hope to create coral gardens in their village waters.

Although the Coral Triangle faces multiple dangers, stories like Angelique's, Nicole's, and Helen's offer hope. "There are so many people working for our ocean, and that brings me great joy," Annie says. "Community members, scientists, and even children are involved."

But on a recent dive in Indonesia, Annie filmed a sea turtle "posing" for her and noticed a piece of plastic fishing line sticking out of its cloaca, or bottom. "I tried to pull out the line, but it was stuck inside with what felt like a hook," she said. "My camera lets me document this so everyone will care and take action. We are the problem, but we are also the solution."

Dive in with Annie to witness her encounter with the turtle.

IN THEIR OWN WORDS: DERYA AKKAYNAK

Turkish scientist Derya Akkaynak and marine biologist Roger Hanlon use Annie's dive skills, her knowledge of coral reefs, and her imaging and storytelling skills during their fieldwork. They study how octopuses, cuttlefish, and squid camouflage themselves. Although Annie's images provide valuable information, they also add to the workload. "We end up analyzing the majority of these images manually, which is time-consuming and expensive," Derya says.

What if scientists could work faster?

Derya (whose name means "ocean" in Turkish and Farsi) has invented a brilliant new way to speed up the study of underwater images. With degrees in aerospace engineering, mechanical engineering, and oceanography, Derya developed a computer program called Sea-thru. Her program removes the water from the underwater images to help scientists clearly identify and examine all the marine life in them.

"It sounds like magic, right?" Annie says. "But Derya is pushing the boundaries of photography."

Other scientists have tried and failed because their math was based on the way light moves through the atmosphere, not the ocean. "A colleague and I showed light moves through the ocean differently and we derived new math," Derya says. "It's hard for me to say this about our work, but it's revolutionary."

Derya hopes to turn scuba divers and snorkelers with cameras into citizen scientists documenting underwater life and changes in our sea, as Annie does. "We'll learn things about the ocean faster and we'll be able to develop solutions faster," she says. "Then we will be able to unleash sophisticated and advanced machine learning on these images so they won't take years and years to process."

CHAPTER 2
THE SALISH SEA:
OUR CONNECTION IS REAL

LONG BEFORE COMPANIES SUCH AS AMAZON, MICROSOFT, AND STARBUCKS CALLED THE PACIFIC NORTHWEST HOME, colliding tectonic plates and slow-moving glaciers carved out three underwater valleys: the Puget Sound in Washington, the Strait of Georgia in Canada, and the Strait of Juan de Fuca on the US-Canadian border. Incoming tides from the neighboring Pacific Ocean mix with fresh water from thousands of snow-fed rivers that empty into the valleys to create an inland waterway known as the Salish Sea.

For thousands of years, the Coast Salish peoples relied on the abundance of life in these emerald waters. They fished for iridescent salmon, silvery herring, multicolored flying sea scallops, and red octopuses. They dug for white-gray clams and harvested gray-green oysters and black mussels on the muddy shore. These and thousands of other marine animals and plants sustained the Salish Sea ecosystem and its people.

Fast-forward two hundred years to the present day. More than eight million people live in the

Salish Sea region and are reminded of their connection to it every day. Multiple bridges cross rivers and bays. Boats ferry people to the many islands along the winding coastline. The region supports many of the world's most important fisheries, which feed millions of people. Scuba divers, ferry boat captains, tour guides, scientists, and many others make their living from the bounty and the beauty of these waters.

Although the Salish Sea is much colder than the Coral Triangle, phytoplankton at the bottom of the food web support all the life in both ecosystems. Huge numbers of these tiny plants tint the Salish Sea green. Most are so small that one hundred could fit across the width of one human hair. Similar to the zooxanthellae inside coral polyps, phytoplankton soak up carbon dioxide and the sun's energy during photosynthesis to make food and release oxygen. Phytoplankton are the most abundant of all life in the ocean, and they make about half of the oxygen we breathe. "Every breath we take connects us to the sea," Annie says. "We are taught in school that oxygen comes from trees and plants, but that's only part of the story."

Most of us don't know that phytoplankton have been making oxygen nearly 1.7 billion

The Salish Sea Basin boundary

Strait of Georgia

Vancouver Island

Mount Baker

Strait of Juan de Fuca

Puget Sound

Olympic Peninsula

Pacific Ocean

Seattle

Area shown

Mount Rainier

Miles
0   25   50

Join Annie's Dive Team on an underwater tour of the Salish Sea.

years longer than plants on land. Without them, our planet could not support human life. Phytoplankton grow and are eaten almost immediately by zooplankton, tiny animals in the next layer of the food web. Small fish gobble the zooplankton, big fish eat the small fish, and even bigger fish eat the big fish.

Along with phytoplankton, salmon top the list of important species in the Salish Sea. Anyone who lives in the area knows these remarkable fish form the backbone of the ecosystem. They migrate from fresh water to salt water and back to fresh water. Young salmon hatch in one of the region's many rivers. On their race to the sea, they become food for larger fish and birds. Many salmon that make it to the ocean are eaten by whales, orcas, seals, sea lions, and us. After one to four years at sea, the surviving salmon do an about-face and travel hundreds or thousands of miles back to the freshwater streams where they were hatched. In these streams, bears and eagles prey on them. Salmon that live long enough to spawn—lay and fertilize their eggs—finally die. Their bodies, which are packed with nutrients from the ocean, fertilize the rivers and forests throughout the Pacific Northwest.

Annie lives on the coast of the Puget Sound. "Everyone is awed by Seattle's Space Needle as a miracle of engineering," she says. "And we can't imagine life without Starbucks or Amazon. But few see our deep connection to what lies below the surface of the water."

To highlight this connection, Annie's photos not only capture the diversity of underwater life, but they also capture change—obvious change, such as sea stars dying in warming seas, and

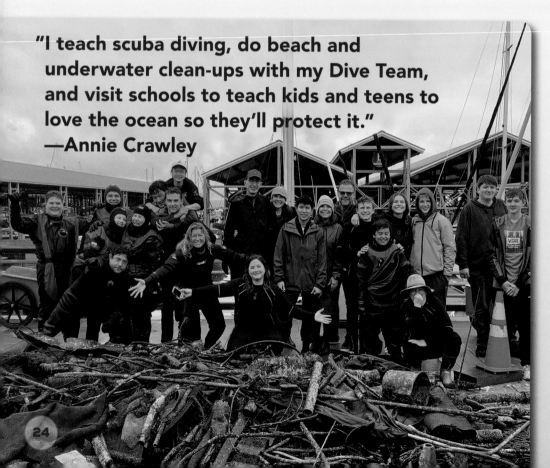

"I teach scuba diving, do beach and underwater clean-ups with my Dive Team, and visit schools to teach kids and teens to love the ocean so they'll protect it."
—Annie Crawley

not-so-obvious change, such as ocean acidification. Pacific Northwest fish and shellfish may feed millions of people, but the ecosystem is stressed. "These changes are hard to get people to connect to," Annie says. "Although they're happening in our backyard, they're happening below the surface."

While these harmful changes aren't visible to most people, scientists such as Meg Chadsey are paying close attention. Meg is the ocean acidification expert at Washington Sea Grant in Seattle, which helps protect marine ecosystems and encourages people to use them responsibly.

We already saw how ocean acidification harms coral reefs. It disturbs shellfish and other animals in the Salish Sea in a similar way.

"When a baby oyster hatches, it survives on the yolk 'sack lunch' from its mother for its first two days of life," Meg says. During that time, the

In second grade Annie learned the oxygen we breathe comes from trees and plants on land. But learning to scuba dive after college completed the picture. "I discovered most of our oxygen comes from plants in the ocean," she says.

baby needs to build a shell to live in so it can feed itself. "Carbonate ion in seawater is critical for shell-making," she says. But in acidified seawater, the additional acid molecules trap available carbonate ion so the baby oyster can't use it. The young oyster must work harder and longer to find carbonate ion, and it can starve before it finishes building its shell.

As if the baby oyster doesn't already have enough trouble, cold currents well up from deep in the Pacific Ocean. This cold water stores tons and tons of carbon—some from natural sources,

OCEAN ACIDIFICATION

CO_2 enters the ocean from the atmosphere.

CO_2 combines with H_2O to form carbonic acid.

Carbonic acid releases H+.

H+ quickly combines with the carbonate ion in seawater.

But coral and shellfish also need carbonate ion to grow. Increased CO_2 levels in the ocean mean less carbonate ion is available to them.

KEY
CO_2 (carbon dioxide)
H_2O (water)
H_2CO_3 (carbonic acid)
H+ (hydrogen ion)
CO_3^{-2} (carbonate ion)

but more and more from our carbon pollution. As a result, the water has already been acidified.

But the trouble doesn't stop there. "Nitrogen and phosphorus from our farms, lawns, and dog-poop-filled sidewalks as well as from most sewage treatment plants can make ocean acidification worse," Meg says.

The combination of acidified water and pollution often kills young oysters as well as other shellfish such as crabs, clams, and mussels. The birds, fish, and marine mammals throughout the food web that eat shellfish will either learn to eat something else—or go hungry and eventually die. People who work in the shellfish industry will lose their jobs. Many shellfish that manage to survive ocean acidification may be unsafe to eat. The extra nitrogen and phosphorus in the water fertilize algae blooms, and some of these algae make toxins that accumulate in the shellfish.

Shellfish aren't the only marine life in the Salish Sea bothered by ocean acidification and pollution. Salmon struggle too. The number of adult salmon returning from the ocean to spawn has plummeted. Scientists know salmon use their sense of smell to find their way home. But in laboratory experiments using acidified water, a juvenile salmon's sense of smell goes haywire. They could not smell their predators. Because wild salmon are extremely hard to test, scientists still have a lot of questions. "Will adults be able to find the food they need to eat or smell the predators trying to eat them?" Meg asks. "If they can't smell their way home, will that affect their ability to spawn? No one knows."

Annie introduces us to the complex web of land and marine life supported by the Salish Sea.

IN THEIR OWN WORDS: IRIS KEMP

"Salmon are the lifeblood of the Salish Sea," Iris Kemp says, and she is on a mission to save them.

In seventh grade, Iris decided to become a marine biologist even though her South Carolina hometown was hours from the ocean. "I read—a lot. And I read biographies of scientists—a lot," she says. In college she took a fish biology course and was hooked. "These creatures are so different from us and we depend on them for so many different things," Iris says.

In graduate school at the University of Washington, Iris found her life's work. "I fell in love with salmon and the way they connect [river, Salish Sea, and marine] ecosystems and provide us with food and cultural experiences," she says. "Basically, our entire Pacific Northwest experience depends on salmon."

Iris works with Long Live the Kings, a group of scientists and environmentalists trying to understand the role salmon play in the Salish Sea. "How energy moves from the base of the food web up to apex predators, like [orcas]," Iris says. "How altering those linkages can change the entire ecosystem. And what we might expect in the future under these really uncertain scenarios of climate change, ocean acidification, and a rapidly growing Puget Sound population."

While science marches on, members of the Lummi Nation mourn the lack of salmon. For centuries these Coast Salish people have called themselves the Salmon People because of their dependence on salmon fishing.

"We lived our lives around salmon," says Dana Wilson, a Lummi elder fisherman. "We migrated with them. Salmon are who we are—our economy, our trade, our songs and dances. It's how we always sustained ourselves." According to Lummi culture, the salmon's migration symbolizes the struggle that makes life worthwhile. The annual Lummi salmon ceremony used to give thanks for the abundance of salmon.

"At the ceremony I attended," Annie says, "the Lummi prayed for the salmon's return. For the first time in his life, Dana is not fishing for salmon because not enough of them are returning."

One hundred years ago, Chinook (also called king) salmon weighed about 100 pounds (45 kg) each. "I've been on the water for the past fifty years," Dana says. "I look back at old photos and my grandfather caught 40- to 50-pound [18 to 23 kg] salmon. My father caught 25-pound [11 kg] salmon. I averaged 18 pounds [8.2 kg]. My son catches 10- to 12-pound [4.5 to 5.4 kg] fish. How's an orca going to survive on a 10- or 12-pound salmon? Salmon are the basis of the Salish Sea. If we can't go out and

Top: The Lummi use traditional methods to cook salmon for their salmon ceremony.
Bottom: Dana Wilson (*right*) hauls in his net.

catch fish, it affects our way of life, our health, our spirituality. Without them we'll lose everything."

The Lummi people aren't the only ones in danger of losing everything. All the people and animals of the Pacific Northwest will suffer too. Orcas are the largest predators in the Salish Sea, but they're suffering because their favorite food, Chinook salmon, is struggling. Noise pollution from ships may harm the orcas' ability to find food. Poisonous chemicals from runoff and floating plastic probably make orcas and salmon sick. Sick animals often don't feel like eating. Animals that don't eat die. We know that healthy predators signal healthy ecosystems. If the Salish Sea can't support its orcas, will it be able to support all the other living things that depend on it?

The Salish Sea is the phytoplankton, the salmon, oysters, clams, and crabs, the orcas, bears, and eagles. It's Dana, Annie, and all the people of the Pacific Northwest. Their hearts beat to the rhythm of its waves. "Most of us believe we have no immediate connection to the changes in the Salish Sea." Annie says. "But our connection is real."

The Lummi Nation feels it, and so must we before salmon and shellfish disappear, and with them orcas, bears, birds, the forest, and everything else in the food web. Let's be the force of change and encourage business and government leaders to make eco-friendly choices. Then ask ourselves a simple question: What changes can we make to our own habits to keep our ocean—and us—healthy?

MAKING WAVES: KALIL ALOBAIDI

"When I teach kids and teens to scuba dive, I'm trying to create life-long ocean stewards," Annie says. "Stewards who take an active role in protecting what they love. Every single one of them becomes a piece of my blue heart."

Seventeen-year-old Kalil Alobaidi, one of Annie's Dive Team members, spoke to the Washington House Environment and Energy Committee to convince them to ban plastic bags statewide.

"I've seen so much beauty right here in our very own Puget Sound but I would be lying if I told you that beauty is the only thing I've seen underwater," said Kalil, who started diving with Annie when he was thirteen. "Last year, I participated in an ocean clean-up in my local port of Edmonds and it broke my heart to see our ocean floor littered with single-use plastic.

"I speak in front of you today, not only . . . for scuba divers across Washington, but for the youth in our state who don't have the ability to vote. It is ultimately . . . the kids of future generations who will have to live with the consequences of an unhealthy environment. . . . We have to continue to influence public policy to raise awareness about environmental issues because if we progress at this current pace without any changes, there might not be an ocean . . . to fight for in the future."

See Kalil (*second from left*) in action. His speech helped convince Washington to approve a plastic bag ban.

CHAPTER 3
THE ARCTIC:
THE TOP OF THE WORLD

ABOVE THE ARCTIC CIRCLE, NATURE PAINTS THE WORLD WITH SHADES OF WHITE THAT HIDE THE LINE BETWEEN LAND AND SEA. The Arctic is as magical as it is foreign, with a silence so intense it seems to shout. On land, only a thin layer of tundra thaws each season. Under the tundra's grasses, most of the ground remains permanently frozen as permafrost. Braided streams of water flow over the permafrost from the mountains to the sea. From above, ocean, land, lakes, and rivers create a lacy web. The sea's massive ice sheets partially thaw during the short summer and refreeze in winter.

Annie first explored the region by ship from Svalbard, Norway. "The Arctic is alive in a way most of us have never before experienced," she says. "It blew my mind that I was at the top of the world!" Aboard the ship she heard summer ice bang against the hull, and the slow *cra-a-a-a-a-ck* and *pop!* of moving ice. "Then you hear the cry of birds called kittiwakes," she says. "As the boat moves between pieces of floating ice, it exposes fish and other creatures these gulls feed on."

Even in this icy wonderland, a food web exists. It begins with ice algae, plants that thrive under several feet of ice. Like the phytoplankton that feed the Coral Triangle and the Salish Sea, ice algae feed the Arctic. But they are different too. They grow in low light and provide fats rich in nutrients and calories, often the difference between life and death for fish and mammals in this harsh environment.

Tiny shrimplike krill feast on ice algae. Krill then become food for the massive humpback, blue, and bowhead whales. Squid and fish such as salmon and halibut also swallow krill and are then eaten by narwhals, beluga whales, seals, walruses, and polar bears.

In the Coral Triangle and the Salish Sea, the effort to eat and avoid being eaten is on display for anyone with a snorkel or an air tank. But the Arctic food web is not as easy to see. "In Indonesia, I wear the ocean. It becomes part

Visit the top of the world with Annie, and see beneath the ice.

of me," Annie says. "But in the Arctic, there's a layer between me and the water." Covered head to toe in a drysuit, only Annie's face is exposed to the frigid water. Below the ice everything moves slowly—kelp, fish, and even Annie.

Wind, temperature, and the saltiness of the water drive a global ocean conveyor belt that moves seawater around the planet. This conveyor belt normally replenishes the world's ocean—from the Arctic to the Coral Triangle and the Salish Sea—with cold, oxygen-rich Arctic water ideal for healthy food webs. But as the ocean absorbs more carbon dioxide, its ability to hold on to oxygen decreases. Less oxygen in seawater means less oxygen for marine life to breathe.

Onshore in Utqiaġvik, Alaska, Annie meets the Iñupiat people. These Alaskan Natives have explored and thrived in the Arctic for centuries by

"Tune into your environment. That's when your mind opens to the signs around you. By getting quiet and becoming part of nature, we learn so much."
—Annie Crawley

using sea ice as land. Prior to the 1800s, Iñupiat lives moved with the rhythms of the seasons on the land they called *nuna*. They traveled between the coast and the Alaskan interior, following whale and caribou migrations.

Respect for nature is one of the traditional Iñupiat values. They admire polar bears, foxes, and snowy owls because these animals have skills mere humans lack. The Iñupiat succeed in the Arctic because, through centuries of trial and error, they developed a huge storehouse of knowledge about their surroundings. Their close relationship with nature has enabled them to survive and protect the land and ecosystems on which they rely.

George Edwardson, a former geologist and current Iñupiat community elder, introduced Annie to Utqiaġvik. He recalled his parents' stories of living in sod houses with whalebone roofs. Resources from land and sea provided everything the family needed. One bowhead whale, loaded with protein and vitamins, fed thousands of people and supplied cooking and heating oil. Because there are no trees, bones became building materials. "There were no roads and no electricity," George says. "People heated their homes with [drift]wood or coal and lit their homes with [seal oil

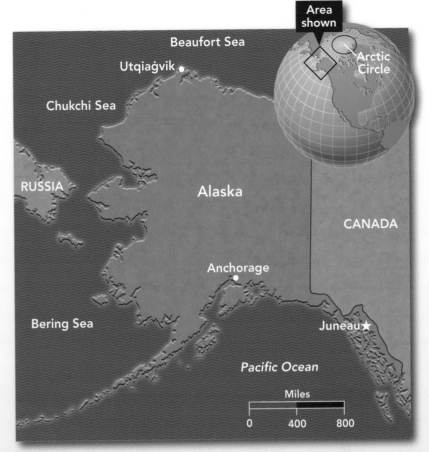

lamps]." To this day, they have no dairy cows for milk or cheese, and no farms or backyard gardens with fresh vegetables. For fruit, they still pick wild salmonberries and blueberries. Vegetables include roots, seaweed, and the bark of shrubs.

In 1971, the US passed a new law that required Alaskan Natives in the north to turn over 90 percent of their lands, including many important hunting and cultural grounds. In return, the government paid a cash settlement to newly formed regional and village Alaska Native corporations. According to George, these events "turned the Iñupiat from a people who depended entirely on the land to a people who were forced to depend on a cash economy."

This new economy allowed oil companies to pay the Iñupiat a fee for the right to search for oil on the remaining Iñupiat lands. Oil companies provided paying jobs, roads, electricity, and other modern conveniences. Wealth from oil gave the Iñupiat new opportunities, but it also led them further from their traditional way of life.

The world's voracious appetite for oil destroys the ice on which the Iñupiat depend. Ice used to start melting in the middle of July and refreeze in August. Lately, because of our changing climate, the ice melts as early as February and doesn't refreeze until December. And when it does refreeze, it's thinner and more dangerous for the Iñupiat to cross. Summer temperatures used to reach a high of 47°F (8.3°C). In June 2020, the temperature in one Arctic town soared to 100°F (38°C)! The heat is melting the permafrost—ground that has been permanently frozen for millennia.

Polar bears hunt from ice floes like this one. As the ice melts, they come ashore far from their hunting grounds where they must survive for long periods of time without food.

MAKING WAVES: EBEN HOPSON

Eben Hopson stands at the northernmost tip of the US next to the lower jawbone of a bowhead whale. Waves roll onto the rocky beach, and a salty tang spices the air. Normally, ice covers the shore and protects the coastline from storms and erosion. But the ice is melting earlier than ever and makes the spring whaling season more difficult.

"Seeing how climate change affects my people scares me," Eben says. "What will the ice be like for future spring whale hunts? My people depend on the ice [to hunt] for food such as seals, polar bear, and bowhead whales."

In high school, Eben experimented with photography and film, and in 2017, he started his own film company. "I thought we needed more native voices in media and media production, so I make films about my hometown and my state featuring native peoples," Eben says.

In October 2017, Eben became an Arctic Youth Ambassador at the age of eighteen. The program accepted a diverse group of students from all over Alaska to represent their hometowns nationally and internationally. "The program helped me put a voice to what I wanted to express through text and film,"

he says. "I traveled the world and showed my films while talking about how the changing climate has negatively affected my town."

Eben has found his purpose. "I am trying to create awareness about what we as a coastal community will face in the coming years," he says. And the community is listening. Local organizations have hired him to produce more films about environmental changes in northern Alaska. With each film, Eben stays true to the Iñupiat voice inside him that says he must protect the world around him.

The frozen ocean that used to sustain the Iñupiat now drowns the land beneath their feet. The shoreline of George's childhood is underwater. Fifty years ago, the Iñupiat became climate refugees and began moving the town of Utqiaġvik (formerly named Barrow) farther inland one level at a time to escape rising seas. Within the next ten years, parts of the town must move again.

Shore-fast ice—ice that forms on the coast and extends into the sea—used to protect the coastline from fall storms. As it disappears, storm waves regularly wash away the beach. The Iñupiat must pack sandbags along the shoreline to protect their homes.

The lost ice makes the Arctic the most visually dramatic place to observe the devastating effects of climate change. "The Arctic is climate change in real time," Annie says. "The melting ice is not just changing this habitat. It impacts every one of us around the world, including the Coral Triangle and the Salish Sea."

The massive loss of ice driven by climate change has forced the Iñupiat to adapt their centuries-old whaling traditions. Historically, men dug a path through the ice to the sea.

In Utqiaġvik, George (*right*) feels the effects of climate change every day. Even though the Iñupiat build homes on stilts to protect the permafrost, warming temperatures turn permafrost into puddles.

They carried their boats from the village to their base camp at the edge of the ice about 2 feet (0.6 m) above open water. There they'd wait for whales to swim along the coast, usually within 10 miles (16 km) of base camp. Because of sea level rise and the lack of shore-fast ice, the distance between whaling crews and whales has grown. The Iñupiat must paddle 40 to 60 miles (64 to 97 km)—or use gasoline-powered motorboats—to find a whale. After a successful harpoon strike, villagers must work fast to tow the 100-ton (91 t) animal four to six times farther to shore, and still harvest, distribute, and store the meat within twenty-four hours before it begins to rot.

Even if we all stopped burning fossil fuels today, the melting ice has launched a vicious cycle that's difficult to stop. When ice melts, it becomes water. Water absorbs heat faster than ice, which increases ocean surface temperatures. Warmer water temperatures make more ice melt. And although less ice allows krill to reach ice algae more easily, once the ice disappears, so does the algae. When the algae vanish, the food web no longer sustains the ecosystem. Salmon (some of which migrated from the Salish Sea), whales, polar bears, walruses, seals, and the Iñupiat will have a lot less to eat. Without ice algae and other necessary organisms, Arctic waters might not be

As shore-fast ice disappears, Iñupiat use sandbags to protect their town from rising sea levels. Their knowledge of Arctic ice goes back generations, and they help scientists understand its history.

able to replenish nutrients in the Coral Triangle or the Salish Sea, further damaging those food webs.

Disappearing ice also opens the Arctic to more traffic including ships searching for oil, fishing vessels, and ships carrying tourists. These ships bring new dangers to the ecosystem. For instance, oil company ships tow seismic air guns to search for oil and natural gas beneath the ocean floor. Underwater, the air gun blasts sound as loud as a jet engine taking off and can be heard nearly 2,500 miles (4,023 km) from the ship—every ten seconds around the clock for weeks. These blasts have many consequences. They kill zooplankton and interfere with the echolocation that animals such as whales and dolphins use to communicate and find food.

More than two-thirds of all seafood caught in the US comes from Alaskan waters. But as more ice melts, pressure mounts to fish waters that used to be impossible to reach. A whopping sixty-four thousand colossal fishing boats sail the high seas worldwide. These boats measure more than 78 feet (24 m) long and drag nets along the ocean floor that are big enough to scoop up twelve jumbo jet airplanes at once. Each year

This ship carrying tourists breaks through ice in its path.

these boats damage an area of ocean floor equal to twice the size of the US. And about half the fish they catch is unused and goes to waste. For centuries our fish supply seemed endless, but because of our unsustainable fishing practices, we've removed them from the ocean faster than they can reproduce.

George is worried. "I need help protecting the ocean," he says. He sees how the world's fish supply is strained from overharvesting and pollution. "Whales depend on krill and fingerlings [young fish]. Eagles can't live without fish. The bears, the walruses, all the marine mammals— that's their food. The only job I have now is to fight to protect my home, the way I live, my language, and the animals I eat," he says. And he wants us to join that fight.

The melting Arctic ice affects every one of us around the world, and there is no global plan to stop it. About twenty years ago Annie met Angaangaq Angakkorsuaq, a traditional healer, shaman, and storyteller from Greenland who helped her understand how important her voice was for our ocean. According to his Inuit traditions, people are the custodians of Mother Earth. "He said his people had been talking about the melting Arctic ice since the 1960s, but no one was listening," Annie says. "He said he'd have to melt the ice in the heart of man before people would address carbon pollution and climate change. I feel the same way."

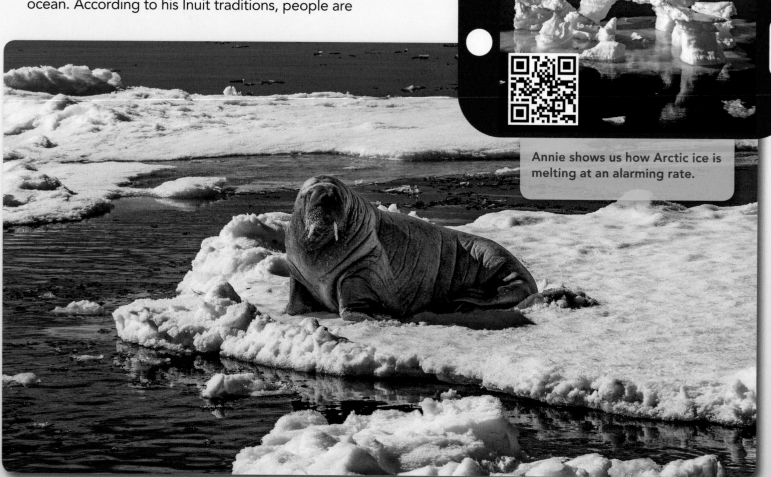

Annie shows us how Arctic ice is melting at an alarming rate.

IN THEIR OWN WORDS: JAMES BALOG

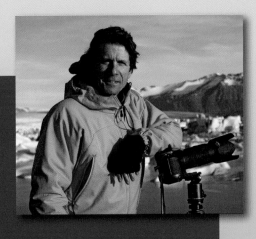

Like Annie, Colorado photographer James Balog records change with images. "As an artist, I have a basic human desire to pay attention to the world around me," he says. A magazine assignment to photograph Iceland's glaciers combined with his experience as a mountaineer sparked his Extreme Ice Survey. "Ice sheets hundreds of thousands of years old were breaking up," Jim says. "Climate change was something I needed to deal with."

Jim challenged himself to make the invisible visible. He built time-lapse cameras tough enough to withstand below-zero temperatures and severe winds.

"I personally obsessed over every nut, bolt, and washer in these crazy things," he says. Jim and a team of assistants hiked, skied, and dogsledded to glaciers in seven areas of the world. They drilled holes in bedrock to keep the cameras from moving with the ice. The cameras snapped photos roughly every thirty to sixty minutes. Through the thirteen field seasons, Jim and his team gathered more than 1.5 million images. They show thinning glaciers, shrinking glaciers and, in some cases, glaciers that have disappeared altogether.

"It's vital to remember that we are part of nature," he says. "Nature isn't some other thing that exists somewhere else. When you assimilate that idea into your heart and your mind and your life, it changes your perspective. You realize that in being kind to nature, you're being kind to yourself."

CHAPTER 4
IT'S YOUR TURN:
THE OCEAN'S STORY
IS OUR STORY

THE OCEAN'S STORY HAS BEEN OUR STORY FROM THE VERY BEGINNING.
Scientists believe life on Earth likely began in its briny depths. Deep-sea hydrothermal vents spout warm, mineral-rich water, which possibly fueled the earliest life. Over billions of years, organisms with one cell evolved into organisms with several cells. Some of those organisms produced oxygen. Early underwater plants, fungi, and animals appeared, followed by early jellies, bony fish, and sharks. About five hundred million years ago while fish were evolving in the sea, early animals came ashore and plants started to grow on land. Several mass extinctions wiped out much of the life in the sea and on land, including dinosaurs. But life endured. The ocean powered its survival.

The ocean's richness continues to make our world possible. It makes *us* possible through the oxygen, water, and food it provides. After visiting the Coral Triangle, the Salish Sea, and the Arctic, we better understand that the ocean also fills our souls. Science recently discovered what divers, water

skiers, swimmers, sailors, surfers, boogie boarders, and paddleboarders have known all along—the ocean soothes us and boosts our creativity.

If humans disappeared off the face of the planet tomorrow, the ocean would heal itself over time. The ocean doesn't need us, but we need the ocean. Try to imagine life without a healthy ocean. How would we breathe? How would we eat or drink? Could we survive?

"We live in an absolutely incredible world which exists because of our ocean," Annie says. "But it is misunderstood, misrepresented, and undervalued by our society. Many of us fear the water and don't see past the surface. Yet the ocean is us. What we do on land impacts our source of life. Every drop of water we drink and much of the food we eat starts with the sea. Breathe in and you breathe ocean."

IN THEIR OWN WORDS: STELLA SUNG

While visiting the New England Aquarium, composer Stella Sung learned about noise pollution from seismic air guns searching for oil beneath the ocean floor. "As a musician . . . it was overwhelming to me that anything could be that loud and that constant," Stella says. The experience planted the seed for a new symphony. *Oceana* harnesses the passion and flexibility of music to increase awareness about how human noise influences marine life. "This is an important work for me as a composer," says Stella, who had never before written music to prompt change.

A friend introduced her to Annie, and they bonded over their shared desire to educate people of all ages about the importance of the ocean. Stella asked Annie to create a film to run while the eighty members of the orchestra perform *Oceana*. "I love using multimedia in my works," she says. "I find it's a compelling way to bring music into focus."

Stella uses a variety of orchestral instruments to suggest the beauty and vastness of the sea. "For example, the harp creates undulations and sounds that are sort of wavy," she says. Annie's film adds extra emphasis with video clips of a mother and baby humpback whale, gyrating schools of sardines, and swaying anemones. "I built a marine life soundtrack using the songs of whales, bearded seals, and dolphins that plays under the music," Stella says. Then jarring chords, clanking anvils, and booming drums mimic the air guns these animals must hear. Annie's film shows how humans leave their mark on the sea with plastic, noise pollution, and carbon pollution. Near the end of the piece, the warmth of the strings and whale sounds return us to the ocean's beauty. But there's a warning, too, as Annie's images alternate between humpbacks and smokestacks, patrolling sharks and fish trapped in abandoned nets, and soaring sea turtles and ocean plastic.

"Our collaboration was a special and extraordinary experience," Stella says.

Angelique's story in the Coral Triangle, Dana's in the Salish Sea, and George's in the Arctic demonstrate the pressures and the realities of lives dependent on nature. Their stories also show that *we* are dependent on nature, specifically the sea. Scientists have proven our habits harm the ocean, but our current politicians cannot agree on how to make the necessary changes. "Rather than wait for them to figure it out, we must make choices that heal the ocean," Annie says. "You, your parents, friends, teachers, grandparents, librarians—all of us who understand must share how the ocean's story is our story."

So what do we do? As readers, we know stories in books have the power to spark change. The same is true for our stories. We have powerful storytelling tools on our smartphones and tablets that we can use to educate and inspire, just as Annie does.

"We are story-making machines," Annie says. "We need to start with what we're passionate about. Our voices have power." Maybe it's

What sort of story might Alex Peijs tell about swimming through a kelp forest?

dolphins, sharks, or turtles. Maybe we want to ban single-use plastic or support renewable energy or encourage family members and friends to support community leaders who speak up for the environment. "I want you to find your voice," Annie says. "What you say and think matters."

The key is to craft our stories so others listen and are inspired to act. The many children, teens, and adults in the pages of this book have answered the call to action, and empower us to speak up and follow their lead. Through action, we find our voices.

MAKING WAVES: AJI PIPER

"I'm not fighting climate change, I'm fighting for human change," says nineteen-year-old Aji Piper. At the age of twelve, Aji joined Plant-for-the-Planet, an organization committed to planting one *trillion* trees worldwide (they're at 13.5 billion so far).

Aji and twenty other young people also sued the US government to force it to create a plan to combat climate change. "The government has a constitutional obligation to protect natural resources as fundamental rights for current and future generations," Aji says. "It has known for fifty years that fossil fuels cause irreversible damage to the climate. Our case is about the federal government's policies that promote fossil fuels, which they understand are destroying the environment."

Aji and his friends lost their case, but because of them, thousands more people are aware of the harmful effects of climate change. We win when we raise our voices.

Aji continues to think globally and act locally. "I'm using the problem of climate change to catalyze shifts in our way of thinking about the planet we live on, the places we live in, and the people we live with."

He plants trees. He speaks out. He shows young people they have more power than they think

they do. "Adults have the responsibility to pick up the burden of climate change because they have more life experience, but kids have power on an emotional scale. They have the power to affect the hearts of the people around them."

Dana Wilson of the Lummi Nation never used to speak to the outside world about his tribal lore and the importance of salmon to his culture. The lack of salmon changed his mind. He now raises his voice to share Lummi knowledge of salmon with storytellers like Annie hoping to trigger change.

Elizabeth Zajaczkowski, a member of Annie's Dive Team, attended a city council meeting in Edmonds, Washington. The city planned to sink concrete pillars for an overpass into the beach of the Dive Team's favorite underwater park. In her speech, she said, "For years other people have represented me, but now that I'm eighteen I'm talking to you as a registered voter. I represent my Dive Team along with other kids and teens in the community who love the ocean [but] are unable to vote. It is important to us that our elected officials

Annie teaches her Dive Team to become ocean storytellers. Nico Ponnekanti (*right*) asks us to go deeper than the surface.

hear our concerns and protect the environment we care about." Thanks to Elizabeth and others like her, the city voted against the new bridge, saving the beach and Edmonds Underwater Park.

Ryan Trotter, a twelve-year old from Chicago, Illinois, took his first underwater breath at Blue Heron Bridge, a magical dive spot off the coast of Florida. Aquarium stores also loved the area. They took—some would say stole—a lot of marine life from its waters to resell to customers.

Divers like Ryan became upset enough to fight for change. They made a video about the problem to educate the public, with Ryan as one of the narrators. He says, "I had the privilege of seeing animals in the ocean, and I want other kids to see them too. They are not just mine or for commercial use. It's our right to have these animals in our world." Because of Ryan and other divers, the marine life at Blue Heron Bridge is protected.

Now it's our turn. It won't be easy. The problems are vast. But we're not alone. We have the support of all the people in this book. Global change starts with stories from our hearts shared again and again. One voice grows into many voices that eventually make a difference. And every success inspires more success.

"We need to remember one important thing about our storytelling," Annie says. "It's not enough that our family and friends know what we think. We have to share our thoughts with people who make decisions—the business and political leaders of our towns, cities, and states. Think hard. We all have a story to tell. What's yours?"

People often draw an invisible line between themselves and nature, but we need to blur that line. "Living for each other is nature's rule," Annie says. "Nothing lives for itself."

By helping the ocean, we help ourselves. Planet Ocean is us.

ANNIE'S PRO TIPS: VISUAL STORYTELLING

"We all have a story to tell," Annie says. "Visual storytelling makes a huge impact and it's all in the palm of your hand. Use these tips and the QR code videos in this book to guide you."

1. Write your story as a narrative or as a video script. Think about the visuals you will need.
2. Practice using your phone, GoPro, or other camera. Know how to focus your scene and how to hold the camera without shaking. Many mobile phones and cameras are waterproof. Consider ways to capture what's happening below the surface in your community.
3. Study the angles in a short video, a photo essay in a magazine, or this book. Count the wide-angle shots, close-ups, and medium shots. Try to figure out why each shot was chosen.
4. Create a list of visuals you'd like for your story.
5. For the best images, put the light source at your back. Early mornings and late afternoons provide warm light for the best outdoor shots.
6. The grid display divides your camera screen into nine boxes that will help you compose shots. For a picture of a friend, line up the eyes with the top grid line. For a sunset, line up the horizon with the bottom grid line.
7. Download and review your images for what works and what doesn't. Reshoot if necessary.
8. Motivate your class to act on behalf of the ocean. Enter contests. Share with the local paper or social media. Use #PlanetOceanBook, and we will boost it.

Dive Team member Abbey Dias shares her ocean story. Watch for camera angles and her overall message.

GO BLUE WITH ANNIE

Imagination is not just child's play; it's for visionaries. Everything from a pencil to a mobile phone started in someone's imagination. The same is true for our dream of a healthy ocean. Your imagination is a vital resource. We need your voice to drive business and policy change. Without you, the ocean has no voice. Here are some things you can do to make a difference:

- **COMMIT TO ZERO WASTE.** Refuse single-use plastic. Pack zero-waste lunches, and use only reusable bottles, grocery bags, and coffee cups. Use soap, shampoo, and conditioner in bar form. Use toothpaste tablets and bamboo toothbrushes. Pack bamboo silverware in your backpacks. Use metal straws. Join or start an environmental team with your classmates to make the changes you want to see at school and in your community.

- **TAKE CLIMATE ACTION.** Walk, ride your bike, carpool, or ride the bus. To save electricity, turn off lights, switch to LED light bulbs, and unplug devices when not in use. Email, call, or attend city council meetings to let them know you care about laws to protect our environment. Research electric vehicles with your parents. Help get electric buses into your community.

- **THINK BEFORE YOU EAT.** Eat more plants and less meat. Go vegetarian for at least one day a week. Eat only fruit and veggies wrapped in their own packaging. Get rid of plastic in your fridge. Use mesh produce bags in the grocery store and beeswax paper instead of plastic wrap. Only use products with sustainable palm oil. Buy only sustainably caught seafood. Reduce food waste. Bring your own containers to the store and restaurant.

- **BE THE VOICE OF OUR OCEAN.** Read books and articles, and talk about the ocean every day. Write poems and stories and make films about how we are connected. Speak up as a role model, and share the ocean's story. Help change plastic policies in local restaurants and local governments. Participate in an ocean, lake, or river cleanup. Join a climate, science, or ocean march.

A NOTE FROM THE AUTHOR AND THE PHOTOGRAPHER

We've been friends for a long time. We met while creating the book *Plastic, Ahoy! Investigating the Great Pacific Garbage Patch*. And because we're friends, we like to work together. It seemed only natural to combine our talents in a book about our relationship to the sea. But where to begin? The ocean is vast, right?

It made the most sense to highlight different areas of our unique and beautiful ocean to show how interconnected we are with it. We also liked the visual contrast between these three areas and how they represent diverse yet connected ecosystems.

Annie was born and raised in Chicago, Illinois. She competed on swim teams and swam in Lake Michigan. After college, she learned to scuba dive and sail, and it changed her life. For the past twenty-five years she's traveled, worked, and lived around the world as an underwater photographer and filmmaker. She actually sold her car to purchase her first underwater cameras. Now she lives in Seattle at the edge of the Puget Sound area of the Salish Sea but still considers the ocean home.

Patti grew up in Vermont and now lives in Sacramento, California. As a kid, she grew vegetables, planted trees and flowers, and sailed with her dad. Water drew her like a magnet—rivers, lakes, the ocean—and it still does. What better way to show her love of the water than by writing about it?

In January 2019, our editor Carol Hinz at Lerner accepted our *Planet Ocean* proposal (a document that includes an outline of the book). Patti traveled to Seattle in March, where she and Annie took a deep creative dive to figure out how to collaborate on such a colossal subject. We needed to bring *Planet Ocean* into your

hearts and minds, and convince you we are all ocean citizens. We wanted to craft a story that demonstrated our connection to the sea. During planning sessions, we chatted about how to incorporate science, images, storytelling, and the voices of native people into the narrative to demonstrate how ocean changes are already impacting people around the world. Some of these issues are not easy to read about. They are complex and have serious consequences. So we also wanted to empower you to act on behalf of our ocean.

Before Patti left Seattle, Annie introduced her to the Dive Team. Together, they gave Patti a scuba lesson. Because Annie's life and the lives of many of her students changed when they took their first underwater breaths, they wanted to share the experience with Patti so she could write about *Planet Ocean* with a below-the-surface perspective.

Between April and October, Annie traveled to Indonesia, Mexico, California, the Arctic, Tonga, and all around the Pacific Northwest working on images and conducting interviews for *Planet Ocean* to merge storytelling, current science, and community action. Thank goodness for Google Drive and Dropbox! Annie uploaded video and audio files so Patti could watch and listen back in Sacramento.

We've poured all of our passion and love for the ocean into this book. Every person in its pages has some connection to us. Ten years ago, people did not want to talk about ocean pollution. Today countries are banning single-use plastic and our changing climate has sparked a youth movement to change corporate and government policies.

We hope you love reading and exploring *Planet Ocean* as much as we loved creating it. More importantly, we hope it inspires you to share your ocean story with the world. Together, we are the voice for our ocean.

GLOSSARY

carbon: an essential element for life on Earth found in all living plants and animals. Too much carbon causes devastating problems and imbalances in our environment.

carbonate ion: a molecule in seawater that corals need to form hard skeletons and shellfish need to form hard shells

climate change: changes in Earth's weather patterns caused largely by the burning of fossil fuels, such as gasoline

ecosystem: a habitat affected by living factors (plants and animals) and nonliving factors (climate and pollution)

glacier: a massive sheet of ice that slowly moves over hundreds or thousands of years

ice algae: plants that float below sea ice or live within the channels that form when seawater freezes. Ice algae form the base of the food web in the Arctic.

ocean acidification: the result of carbon pollution reacting with seawater that changes the chemistry of the ocean. Coral reefs and shellfish do not grow normally in acidified water. Fish seem to become confused.

phytoplankton: microscopic, single-celled marine plants that form the foundation of the ocean food web

polyp: one of the animals that form a coral reef. Shaped like a cylinder, a polyp is attached to the reef at one end, and the other end is a hollow opening surrounded by tentacles that help draw in food.

salmon: a type of fish that is born in fresh water, migrates to the ocean, and returns to fresh water to spawn (lay or fertilize eggs)

scuba: self-contained underwater breathing apparatus; equipment that uses a portable supply of air for breathing underwater

sea level rise: an increase in the level of the world's ocean due to climate change

seismic testing: a way to search for underground pockets of oil and gas using blasts of sound

symbiotic: living closely together and depending on one another for life. Zooxanthellae and coral polyps have a symbiotic relationship.

tropical ocean: a region that borders the equator. The warm waters of the tropics regulate Earth's climate and weather patterns, and tropical waters are home to much of the ocean's biodiversity.

zooxanthellae: microscopic algae that live inside coral polyps and provide roughly 95 percent of the polyps' energy needs

SOURCE NOTES

7 Annie Crawley, interview with the author, February 22, 2019.

8 Crawley, interview, January 22, 2019; Crawley, manuscript edit, August 1, 2019.

9 Elise Foot Puchalski, Dive Team member, interview with the author, March 5, 2019.

11 Crawley, interview, February 22, 2019.

11 Crawley, manuscript edit, August 22, 2019.

12 Angelique Batuna, owner, Murex Resorts in Manado, on Lembeh Island and Bangka Island, interview by Annie Crawley, May 2019.

12 Batuna.

13 Batuna.

13 Batuna.

14 Crawley, interview, May 26, 2019; Crawley, manuscript edit, August 7, 2019.

16 Batuna, interview.

17 Crawley, manuscript edit, August 13, 2019.

17 Crawley, manuscript edit, July 23, 2019.

17 Crawley, interview, February 22, 2019, and January 22, 2019; Crawley, manuscript edit, August 1, 2019.

18 Helen Pananggung, Green Guru, Lembeh Foundation, interview by Annie Crawley, May 2019.

18 Pananggung.

18 Pananggung.

18 Pananggung.

19 Nicole Helgason, interview with Annie Crawley, May 25, 2019.

20 Crawley, interview, May 26, 2019.

20 Crawley; Crawley, manuscript edit, August 1, 2019.

21 Derya Akkaynak, postdoctoral fellow at Princeton University, interview by Annie Crawley, May 2019.

21 Crawley, interview, May 26, 2019.

21 Derya Akkaynak, "Digitally Draining the Ocean," presentation, Lembeh, Indonesia, May 2019.

21 Akkaynak, interview.

23 Crawley, interview, January 22, 2019.

24 Crawley, interview, March 20, 2019.

24 Crawley, manuscript edit, August 1, 2019.

25 Crawley, interview, January 22, 2019.

25 Meg Chadsey, ocean acidification specialist, Washington Sea Grant, interview by Patricia Newman and Annie Crawley, March 6, 2019.

25 Crawley, interview, January, 22, 2019.

26 Chadsey, interview.

27 Chadsey, email, manuscript edit, July 15, 2020.

27 Chadsey, interview.

28 Iris Kemp, science project manager, Long Live the Kings, interview by Patricia Newman and Annie Crawley, March 7, 2019.

28 Kemp.

28 Kemp.

28 Kemp.

29 Dana Wilson, Lummi Nation elder, interview by Annie Crawley, March 22, 2019.

29 Crawley, text message, November 8, 2019.

29–30 Wilson, interview.

30 Crawley, interview, January 22, 2019, and March 20, 2019.

31 Crawley, interview, January 22, 2019; Annie Crawley, "The past 2 months have absolutely flown or should I say dived by . . . ," Facebook, July 13, 2019, https://www.facebook.com/annie.crawley/posts/10158680857584816.

31 Kalil Alobaidi, email to Annie Crawley with text of speech to the Washington State House Environment and Energy Committee, Olympia, WA, January 21, 2019.

31 Alobaidi.

32–33 Crawley, interview, July 11, 2019.

33–34 Crawley.

34 Annie Crawley, manuscript edit, February 10, 2020.

35 George Edwardson, president, Iñupiat community, interview by Annie Crawley, June 25, 2019.

36 Edwardson, review of manuscript, February 18, 2020.

37 Eben Hopson, Arctic Youth Ambassador, interview by Annie Crawley, June 2019; Hopson, email edits, July 29, 2019.

37 Hopson; Hopson.

37 Hopson; Hopson.

37 Hopson, email to Annie Crawley, July 29, 2019.

38 Crawley, interview, July 3, 2019; Crawley, manuscript edit, August 6, 2019.

41–42 Edwardson, interview.

42 Edwardson.

43 James Balog, founder and director, Earth Vision Institute, interview with the author, April 30, 2019; Balog, *Time-Lapse Proof of Extreme Ice Loss*, performance, TEDGlobal, July 2009, https://www.ted.com/talks/james_balog_time_lapse_proof_of_extreme_ice_loss#t-169091.

43 Balog, *Time-Lapse*.

43 Balog, interview.

45 Crawley, interview, February 22, 2019; Crawley, manuscript edit, August 1, 2019; "Riding the Currents the Realm of the Visionary Underwater Journey by Filmmaker Annie Crawley," YouTube video, 7:56, posted by Annie Crawley, February 20, 2019, https://youtu.be/dxnvEaAWwi0.

46 Stella Sung, composer, interview by Annie Crawley, February 2019.

46 Sung.

46 Sung.

46 Sung.

47 Crawley, interview, January 22, 2020.

47 Crawley, interview, June 19, 2019.

48 Aji Piper, plaintiff, *Juliana v. United States*, interview by Annie Crawley, August 6, 2019.

48 Piper.

48 Piper.

48 Piper.

49–50 Elizabeth Zajaczkowski, Dive Team member, letter to Edmonds (WA) City Council, email to Annie Crawley, June 19, 2019.

50 Ryan Trotter, email, July 22, 2019.

51 Crawley, interview, June 19, 2019.

51 Crawley, interview, February 22, 2019.

52 Crawley, interview, February 22, 2019.

SELECTIONS FROM OUR BIBLIOGRAPHY

Akkaynak, Derya, and Tali Treibitz. "Sea-Thru: A Method for Removing Water from Underwater Images." Paper presented at the 2019 IEEE Conference on Computer Vision and Pattern Recognition, Long Beach, CA, 2019, 1682–1691.

Balog, James, founder and director, Earth Vision Institute. Interview by Patricia Newman, April 30, 2019.

Batuna, Angelique, owner, Murex Resorts in Manado, on Lembeh and Bangka Islands. Interview by Annie Crawley, May 2019.

Cain, Sydney, ASRC, Research and Technology Solutions. Interview by Annie Crawley, March 22, 2019.

Chadsey, Meg, ocean acidification specialist, Washington Sea Grant. Interview by Patricia Newman and Annie Crawley, March 6, 2019.

Crawley, Annie, photographer and filmmaker. Interviews by Patricia Newman, January 22, 2019; February 22, 2019; March 20, 2019; May 26, 2019; June 19, 2019; and July 22, 2019.

Edwardson, George, president, Iñupiat community. Interview by Annie Crawley, June 25, 2019.

Helgason, Nicole, coral gardener. Interview by Annie Crawley, May 2019.

Pananggung, Helen, Green Guru, Lembeh Foundation. Interview by Annie Crawley, May 2019.

Wallace-Wells, David. *The Uninhabitable Earth: Life after Warming*. New York: Tim Duggan Books, 2019.

DIVE INTO THESE OCEAN BOOKS

Eriksson, Ann. *Dive In! Exploring Our Connection with the Ocean*. Victoria, BC: Orca, 2018.
Short chapters and descriptive sidebars explain the science behind our connection to the ocean.

Gaydos, Joseph K., and Audrey DeLella Benedict. *Explore the Salish Sea: A Nature Guide for Kids*. Seattle: Little Bigfoot, 2018.
Tour the Salish Sea and see startling photographs of all the interconnected parts of the region—ocean, marine life, forests, salmon, and people.

Margolin, Jamie. *Youth to Power: Your Voice and How to Use It*. Lebanon, IN: Da Capo Lifelong, 2020.
A teen who has been organizing and protesting since the age of fourteen wrote this inspiring how-to book.

Newman, Patricia, and Annie Crawley. *Plastic, Ahoy! Investigating the Great Pacific Garbage Patch*. Minneapolis: Millbrook Press, 2014.
Three female scientists join the first expedition to the North Pacific central gyre to study how plastic impacts the ocean and the animals that live there.

SURFERS WELCOME

Annie Crawley's *Planet Ocean* Playlist
https://www.youtube.com/user/AnnieCrawley
Watch additional videos from Annie's travels, and behind-the-scenes content about the making of *Planet Ocean*.

"Beat the Uncertainty: Planning Climate-Resilient Cities"
https://games.noaa.gov/beat-the-uncertainty/welcome.html
Players of this online game take on the roles of community leaders in a coastal town to make smart decisions about ways to help the city adapt to climate change.

Climate Kids
https://climatekids.nasa.gov/ocean/
NASA educators answer young readers' climate change questions.

Learn to Scuba Dive!
https://www.padi.com/education
If you're ten years of age or older, you may be able to learn to scuba dive. You'll need to begin with a professional instructor. Check out the Professional Association of Diving Instructors website to find a dive shop near you.

"Nemo on Acid"
https://www.youtube.com/watch?v=wtkDke1EUYE&feature=youtu.be
This animated film explains how carbon pollution endangers clown fish.

Ocean Portal by *National Geographic Kids*
https://kids.nationalgeographic.com/explore/ocean-portal/
Learn more about the sea through ocean animal profiles, challenges, ocean-themed games, videos, and photos.

Sylvia Earle's Hope Spots
https://mission-blue.org/hope-spots/
Sylvia Earle created the idea of Hope Spots to support people trying to protect special places important to the ocean's health. Do you know of a special place that deserves protection? You can nominate your own Hope Spot.

INDEX

acidification, 15, 25, 26–27, 28
activism, 18, 20, 28, 31, 37, 48, 49–50, 53
Akkaynak, Derya, 21
Alobaidi, Kalil, 31
Angakkorsuaq, Angaangaq, 42
Arctic Circle, 6, 32, 35, 44–45, 55
   food web in, 33–34
   melting ice in, 16, 36, 38–40, 42–43

Balog, James, 43
Batuna, Angelique, 12–14, 16–17, 20, 47
Blue Heron Bridge, 50

carbonate ion, 14–16, 26
carbon dioxide, 14–16, 23, 34
carbon pollution, 6, 11, 15, 27, 41–42, 46, 55
Chadsey, Meg, 25, 27
climate change, 15, 28, 37–38, 42–43, 48
climate refugees, 17, 38
Coast Salish peoples, 22–23, 29
coral reefs, 4, 14, 21, 23
   bleaching of, 15–16
   importance of, 10, 17
   restoration of, 16, 19–20
   threats to, 11–13, 15, 17, 20, 25
Coral Triangle, 6, 10–12, 17, 19–20, 23, 38, 44, 47
   food web in, 33–34, 40

Crawley, Annie, 6, 10
   Dive Team, 8–9, 23–24, 31, 49
   philosophy of, 7, 11, 14, 17, 25, 30–31, 34, 38, 45, 47, 51
   photography of, 20–21, 24, 46, 52
   travels of, 29, 32, 34–35, 42

diagrams, 9, 26

Edmonds Underwater Park, 50
Edwardson, George, 35–36, 38, 41, 47
Extreme Ice Survey, 43

fish consumption, 6, 10, 19, 23, 24–25, 27, 33
fishing practices, 11, 17, 20, 22, 29, 40–41
   fish bombing, 13
food web, 6, 23–24, 27–28, 30, 33–34, 39–40
fossil fuels, 15, 39, 48

Great Barrier Reef, 16

Helgason, Nicole, 19, 20
Hopson, Eben, 37

ice algae, 33, 38
Iñupiat people, 34
   climate change and, 38–39
   way of life, 35–37
iron ore mining, 12–13

Kemp, Iris, 28

Lummi Nation, 29–30, 49

mangroves, 12–13
maps, 11, 23, 35
melting ice. *See* rising sea levels

nitrogen, 27

Oceana, 46
oil companies, 12, 36, 40
orcas, 24, 28, 29, 30
oxygen, 5, 16, 23, 34, 44

Pananggung, Helen, 18, 20
permafrost, 32, 36
phosphorus, 27
photosynthesis, 14, 16, 23
phytoplankton, 23–24, 30, 33
Pintu Kota Kecil, 18
Piper, Aji, 48
plastic pollution, 6, 11, 17–18, 20, 30–31, 46–47, 53
political change, 31, 47, 48, 51, 53
Puchalski, Elise Foot, 9

rising sea levels, 39
runoff, 6, 30

Salish Sea, 6, 22–23, 25, 38–40, 44, 47
  food web in, 24, 27–30, 33–34
salmon, 5, 22, 24, 28, 33, 39, 49
  Chinook, 29–30
  sense of smell of, 27
scuba diving, 6, 8, 12, 17, 19–21, 23–25, 31, 44, 49–50
  equipment needed, 9
shellfish, 25, 26, 30
  oysters, 25, 27
storytelling, 6, 8, 11, 20, 21, 23, 35, 42, 44, 47, 49, 51–52, 53
Sung, Stella, 46

tips to help the ocean, 53
tourism industry, 10, 12, 17, 19, 23, 40
Trotter, Ryan, 50

Utqiaġvik, AK, 34–35, 38

Wilson, Dana, 29–30, 47, 49

Zajaczkowski, Elizabeth, 49–50
zooplankton, 24, 40
zooxanthellae, 14, 16–17, 23

ACKNOWLEDGMENTS

A book of this scope would not be possible without friends, colleagues, experts, and young people willing to share their stories. We would like to thank Meg Chadsey, ocean acidification specialist and NOAA Pacific Marine Environmental Lab liaison at Washington Sea Grant; Dana Wilson, elder fisherman of the Lummi Nation; Iris Kemp, senior project manager, Long Live the Kings; Angelique Batuna and Danny Charlton, co-owners, Murex Dive Resorts along with their incredible dive team; Critters at Lembeh Resort; Nicole Helgason, ocean gardener; Derya Akkaynak, PhD, oceanographer, diver, engineer; Roger T. Hanlon, PhD, senior scientist, Marine Biological Laboratory; Sydney Cain, traditional knowledge and native youth advocate, Arctic Slope Regional Corporation (ASRC) shareholder; George Edwardson, elder, Iñupiat community; Stella Sung, composer; James Balog, nature photographer and creator of the Extreme Ice Survey; Helen Pananggung, Lembeh Foundation's inspirational Green Guru; Elise Foot Puchalski, Elizabeth Zajaczkowski, Kalil Alobaidi, Abbey Dias, Nico Ponnekanti, Jaimie Valentine, Tasha Lee, Kai Widmer, and many other members of Annie Crawley's Dive Team; Eben Hopson, Arctic Youth Ambassador and filmmaker; Aji Piper, activist for human change and one of twenty-one plaintiffs in *Juliana v. United States*; Ryan Trotter; and the tireless children of Pintu Kota Kecil who clean up ocean plastic brought in on the tides.

Additional thanks to E. Virginia Armbrust, PhD, professor, School of Oceanography, University of Washington; Michele Hoffman Trotter, founder of Microcosm, college professor; Edi Frommenwiler, captain of the *Pindito* and photographer; Ray Atos, environmental/natural resources director, Iñupiat community of the Arctic Slope; Reanne Tupaaq Johnson, director, Iñupiat History, Language, and Culture Department, North Slope Borough; Jamie Margolin, Zero Hour founder; Steve Woods Photography; Moosa Hassan and Manthiri Maldives; Ernie Brooks, Mike Lever, and Nautilus Liveaboards; Berkley White and Backscatter Underwater Video & Photo; Faith Ortins, Blue Green Expeditions; Rima Deeb Granado, Oceanwide Expeditions; Cody Hurd and Glazers Camera; Camilo Garcia and Divers Underground; Kerri Bingham, Hergen Spalink, Got Muck LLC; Guido Brink, Alison Bygrave, Dewi Nusantara; Marla Kempf, Bob McChesney, and Port of Edmonds Team; Raechel Romero; Pilar Martinelli and Team Unterthiner; Jay Clue, Dive Ninjas; Lucrecia Fabre, Amancay Freediving; Diving Unlimited International; Fourth Element Diving; Light and Motion Dive Lights; Nauticam Underwater Housings; Atomic Aquatics; Zeagle Inc; Aqua Lung; Wanda Narajowski; Harriet Pergande; Terry Keffler and Underwater Sports; Connie Goldsmith, Jeri Chase Ferris, Linda Joy Singleton, and Kendall Newman.